New Year, New Career, New You

Finding Your Dream Job

AARON LITTLES

4

This book is dedicated to my amazing teammate, partner and wife, Madelyn. Without your love, support and patience this book would have never been completed.

Thank you!

Table of Contents

1. Introduction   9

2. Chapter 1: Start with the Dream   13

3. Chapter 2: The WHY   25

4. Chapter 3: The WHAT   31

5. Chapter 4: The HOW   39

6. Conclusion   49

7. Next Steps   53

Introduction

As a small child I was very interested in public speaking. One year in fourth grade I entered an oratorical contest and started my career as a speaker. I gave a passionate and energetic talk about how " Now is the Time" the time for change, the time for us to walk in our purpose, and the time for people to live their dreams. Sadly, I lost (2nd place). I could have asked for a recount, but I gracefully accepted my medal and decided to retire from my new found profession. You see, I tried to live my dream but I "failed" and that small setback could have set me on a tailspin of not trying to achieve future goals. However, my parents encouraged me to try again and again I lost (2nd place to the same kid). I wonder where Rufus is now a days? He had a sermon style of speaking so I hope he is inspiring people every day in the church. I digress. I tell you this story because it would have been very easy for me retire from the lectern for good.

Over the years I realized that second place was actually really good and not just because I beat the third place kid, but because at an early age I overcame a fear that many adults struggle with. I also had a seed be planted deep within me that my purpose was to inspire people to live the life of their dreams.

When I was in high school I was on the track team. We had a scripture that we would say before every meet to get fired up and ready to go. It was Philippians 4:13 "I can do all things through Christ which strengtheneth me" (KJV). As an innocent teenager at a subconscious level I actually believed that statement. I grew up in a house filled with a strong Christian faith. A faith that never wavered during the tough times and was always focused on giving God the glory for our successes and prosperity. I believe it so true when the word says, "Train up a child in the way he should go: and when he is old, he will not depart from it. (Provb 22:6, KJV), even though I grew up in the church and knew Jesus, I went away from what I learned. However, over time I came back to what I was taught. I have been called back to walk the righteous path and fulfill my purpose for the Kingdom.

This book is a testament to that end of walking in the path towards your dream job and dream career. We are all on a path, the question is do you know which way will lead to happiness and prosperity? Secondly, what is holding you back from taking the first step on that path? New Year, New Career, New You is a step towards your preferred future. I look forward to starting the journey with you!

New is exciting. New is scary. New is you, if you want it to be!

Chapter 1: Start with a Dream

Imagine, if you will, a happy employee sitting back in his cushy corner office with a sweet view of (insert an awesome view for yourself mine is Tampa Bay). It's Friday afternoon and this employee has helped the company, been recognized as a valued member of the team and can't wait to get back to the job on Monday. This employee was giving and receiving high fives for the last 20 minutes with everyone on his team after leading the completion of a huge project. Sounds good right? Well what if this was you? What if I said this could be you? Ok, ok I get it, maybe I have painted a perfect picture. This may not be your current situation but I challenge you to consider your final destination.

I am a former United States Marine Corps Captain, but you know how the saying goes..."Once a Marine, Always a Marine." I actually had a glimpse of the dream scenario we just described. Being trusted with the responsibility of leading Marines and serving my country was a truly humbling experience. When I was

17 years old I was presented with a difficult decision. In my left hand was one envelope and in my right another, both were acceptance letters to college. Well, sort of... The letter on the left was a direct entry letter to Florida State University. One childhood dream of being able to do the tomahawk chop and mean it could have been realized! On the right was a bit more mystery and intrigue. The letter was from the Naval Academy Preparatory School in Newport, Rhode Island. Now, I had applied to the United States Naval Academy and this was their consolation prize. You do one year in Newport, get a C average and pass the physical fitness test and then one year later you get a ticket to the big show in Annapolis at the Academy.

Now as a high school kid currently living in the Sunshine state and understanding that FSU was the number 3 party school in the nation at the time and that Rhode Island averaged 3ft of snow each year, my decision was all but made. My mother asked me,

"Well Aaron, what do you want to do with yourself after college?" I replied, "I want to serve my country and travel the world!" Whoops, the gears started turning and I slowly started to realize the point she was about to make. But she sealed the deal with her next question, "Well Aaron" she said, "Where is the best place to do all that from?" I reluctantly replied in my most disappointed non-party, anti-party, the Naval Academy has discipline for breakfast voice..."The Naval Academy."

So after a year of hard time in Rhode Island (and yes it did snow 3ft), I received my appointment to the Naval Academy. After four years in Annapolis, I was selected for the United States Marine Corps (more discipline). This would turn out to be a series of decisions that added to a great foundation that I received as a young man from my parents. Meaning even getting my dream job was a circuitous path that I would not have mapped out on my own. Even though my six and a half years of active duty in the Marines was the toughest, scariest, and exhilarating time in my life that season of the dream eventually ended. Like a horse in the rain "I was rode hard and put away wet." I was experiencing combat fatigue from back to back deployments. I knew that I had served honorably and that I had new dreams, new goals and new direction to pursue. Just understand that you may have a dream, you may achieve your dream and your dream may change. That is OK!

The problem with my transition from the military was that I didn't clearly define what my next dream job was going to be. In actuality, I was running *away* from the military instead of running *towards* my new dream. I knew that I wasn't really looking to deploy again and go back to combat but on the flip side I didn't have a clear vision of what my new goals and dreams were. I was just running away from an old dream. This happens with many veterans and other professionals that say "I'm going to quit this job just to get out...I HATE IT!" They throw their hands up and exclaim "I'm done!" This is a very dangerous and potentially unwise decision, especially if you haven't put a plan in place on where you want to go next. Have you had a chance to consult with God on what he has for you next? Are you sure your work is done in this current situation? Have you been released from the old dream and been given a new calling with direction?

I believe the that our full potential is only unlocked when we have a relationship with Jesus. I had to go on this personal journey of understanding what gifts God had given me, what mission he gave me, and when he wanted me to start taking action. I was struggling through the adjustment from the Marines to Corporate America (different book). Let's just say there are cultural differences between the two organizations. Especially when you could communicate merely through a dialogue of grunts, YUTs and chest expansion. In the corporate setting I found that I was on a new piece of gym equipment called the Cardio-Climber.

18

The Cardio Climber was just this preverbal corporate ladder that you must climb in order to achieve, but I just seemed to be going no where fast. I began to question if I was maximizing my potential in the corporate setting. Sure, I was using a good portion of my skill set, minus the physically demanding rigors of the military or being on call to save the world from Chemical Biological Radiological disaster. But then again, most jobs don't ask you to make those types of commitment. You see, I had lost my sense of purpose because I lost my sense of service. Many people thrive when they feel needed and are serving their fellow man in some way, shape or form. I did not easily recognize how I was serving others by manning my cubicle battle station or (most likely) that I was serving enough people.

Thus began my journey to find my dream job. Part of the conversation when it comes to dream jobs is money. For my wife and I, we realized that debt was going to inhibit us from doing what we wanted too and what we loved. Especially since we started our young marriage with over $115,000 in consumer debt and we didn't even have a mortgage as part of that number! We wanted to get to a place where we didn't have to work for money. So in an effort to be free career wise we took great lengths to become free financially. I stumbled across a podcast with a guy telling people to cut up their credit cards and live debt free. His name was Dave Ramsey, radio show host, speaker, author and financial expert. By following Dave Ramsey's course and after just 2 years and six months we became DEBT FREE! We got rid of student loans, credit cards, paid off a car, paid and closed off store cards too. Even the Victoria Secrets card, that was ok because they still accept cash! Relax I'm married and all the husbands need to make a line item for that place in you budget. Some would say we went crazy getting rid of all that debt, and I would agree. That bold move allowed my wife to leave a job that was making her grow weary and she began writing her first novel.

Now for you, if you could imagine not owing anyone ANYTHING, what would you do everyday? If you didn't owe anyone anything how many bad days at the office would you stand for? How many bad weeks? Months? You get where I'm going here, the goal being to imagine what that dream looks like. I believe that you have a choice. I believe that when your finances are in order and you have some margin, you are in a better position to not only make your career transition, but to also have confidence about your situation during your next hiring process.

I don't believe we are held against our will at our corporate jobs, if you are please contact your HR rep. All kidding aside, WE all have a choice or better stated a responsibility to direct our careers and grow our personal development. When you have your finances in order, you can think more rationally and have an opportunity to hear what God has to say on the matter. We need to be better at managing what we do have versus what we don't. So you see, we can't talk about career items without talking about earning potential.

People come up to me always "complaining" about their level of income. The conversation goes something like "Aaron I need to earn $100K." I ask "why?" The responses varied but almost every answer has some component of maintaining a lifestyle that does not facilitate a healthy environment. People use the luxury items to hid behind a lack of serving or building better community. Additionally, people get very fired up about the opportunity to talk about their dream or how they are planning on achieving the dream. That conversation sounds like "Well Aaron, I'm a (insert boring job)….but I'd rather be (read with excitement and passion) and then (insert awesome dream job). They don't make the move to their dream simply because of their salary. So it is vital that this be part of your understanding, that in order to full your dream your salary may change one way or another.

Whoops, is there anyone else out there raising their hand? This was the case for me. The concern that I had was surrounding my entire thought process regarding money. We can live a better life and work in our dream field, but we just need to come to the understanding that being deeply in debt won't help us get there faster.

This book will dive into three areas for finding your dream job.

- Why

- What

- How

Chapter Notes

What is your dream? How can you find your dream?

_____

_____

_____

_____

_____

_____

_____

_____

_____

_____

_____

_____

_____

_____

_____

_____

Chapter 2: The WHY

The question posed to you is this: "Why are you searching for your dream job?" In other words, there must be a reason or reasons that your current deal is not your dream. I want you to really think about all the reasons why you aren't happy and really spell out what is leading you towards your dream job. Is it your salary? Your hours or work leadership? Is it your location?

Take a minute to really ponder why you aren't happy in your current situation. This is critical so that when a shiny new job or opportunity arises it better not look the same.

Practical Application; Why isn't your current situation your dream job?

_____

_____

_____

_____

_____

_____

_____

_____

_____

_____

Current Job Rating Table

Rating/ Category	Great	Good	Ok	Poor	Get me outta here!
Salary	5	4	3	2	1
Location	5	4	3	2	1
Job	5	4	3	2	1
Boss	5	4	3	2	1
Other 1;_____	5	4	3	2	1
Other 2;_____	5	4	3	2	1

Total; _____

Now if your current jobs rating from the figure above and you are less than 10 or even 8 for that matter, be sure that you capture as much detail as possible so that we don't repeat these same mistakes.

Just to be clear, I want to list a few disclaimers about finding your dream job.

1. I'm not talking about something magical or fictional such as growing wings and becoming a high-end Uber driver. This is a dream that you have the ability to actually achieve.

2. The dream could end up looking different that what you imagined. Your dream may not have all the details worked out but the actual dream opportunity may be dressed in slightly different clothes but is still very distinctly your dream.

3. You may have to WORK really really hard to achieve your dream.

Quote; "I've missed more than 9000 shots in my career. I've lost almost 300 games. 26 times, I've been trusted to take the game winning shot and missed. I've failed over and over and over again in my life. And that is why I succeed."

-Michael Jordan

My pastor said during a Sunday morning message "When you get a mission from God, something so important to do and get done, you won't quit!" We see that MJ had some tough times in his career, but he had a dream and short term failure didn't stop his long term success.

Chapter Notes

What do you need to overcome to achieve your dream?

_____

_____

_____

_____

_____

_____

_____

_____

_____

_____

_____

_____

_____

_____

_____

_____

Chapter 3: The WHAT

We must identify our dream. We have to figure out what God has called us to do each day. We need to have a some idea of what our dream looks like in order to achieve it. When I was going through this process, I found it difficult to nail down what my dream looked like. So with the help of the awesome surroundings of sunny Tampa, FL I found a little piece of heaven in the form of a quiet beach. I started frequenting this spot and spending time doing writing down my skills, talents, passions and abilities. I found that sometimes I couldn't block out the noise and distractions of my life to get fifteen minutes of headspace to even think about my dream job. I developed the 5-5-5 technique.

*Practical Application

Here's how 5-5-5 works;

- 5 Minutes; Peace and Quiet. Literally, just sit there and slow your mind down. No emails, no Twitter, no Facebook, no LinkedIn, nothing! Just sit and hopefully enjoy the scenery you have in front of you.

- 5 minutes; Dreaming. Actively dream like you did when you were 7 years old and nothing was impossible or impractical. If your having trouble dreaming, imagine what life would be like with no payments, no mortgage, and some cash in the bank.

32

- 5 minutes; Capturing. Write down visions, thoughts, ideas, whatever they may be.

If you repeat this process for any amount of time you will find some recurring themes or even clarity on a direction. This method has helped me launch new business ventures and seek out new opportunities to help the world.

My dream of becoming a speaker and an author started with an application with Dave Ramsey's team in Nashville. As part of his 15 year succession plan he wanted to hire 15 personalities who would travel and speak to people about using God's plans for success in all areas of your life and business. Naturally I didn't want to deny Dave the use of my talents and abilities so I applied to his organization. I was quickly told that I wasn't a good enough speaker and I hadn't actually written anything to even be considered a writer. This felt like an unexpected body blow delivered by a prize fighter. Did I quit and drop my microphone and pen? Did I hang up metaphorical cleats? NO! I re-doubled my efforts and began to train and train and train to become better. To become the guy that Dave's organization was looking for. But along the way, I started to think that I may not need Dave anymore. I started to believe that I was good enough to have my own dream and my own business. My journey isn't complete, but the character building session of getting my stomach sent to my liver was one of the most important lessons I've learned. We can't quit when we find out that we have to put in some work to achieve our dream.

*Practical Application

In addition to the 5-5-5 technique I would like to give you another tool to creatively imagine what your dream looks like. As you do your 5-5-5 technique, gather a list of key words that describe you and your dream job. For instance, mine looked something like; leader, communicator, problem-solving, service. You take these key words and plug them into a job search engine and see what job titles pop up. This is cool because you may see something that sparks your interest but that wasn't something you had ever considered doing. For me one of the titles that came up was Disaster Response Coordinator for the Red Cross. Based on my military background and desire to assist people in need this was a cool job that I never even considered before.

List of your key words;

_____

_____

_____

_____

_____

_____

_____

_____

*Practical Application

As you begin to narrow down the list of possible opportunities for yourself you may want to shadow someone for a day. Tell them you are looking into a career change and want to learn more about what they do and would love to experience a day in the life. Don't forget to bribe everyone in the office with coffee and donuts so they tell you The Good, The Bad, and The Ugly! This is an important information gathering situation as you also gain an opportunity to build a relationship with several people in the office. If you are on your LinkedIn game this could prove extremely beneficial. We'll discuss LinkedIn shortly as that tool can be very beneficial in assisting you in the job search and research process.

Script;

You; "Hey Tom!"

Tom; "Hi Aaron!"

You; Additional greeting, like how's the family and such....Tom may be dealing with some life and we want to make sure this is a good time to talk and catch up.

Tom; Thanks for asking we are well...how are you?

You; Well I'm actually in the middle of a career transition. I know you've said some great things about the field your in and I was wondering if.....

Option 1; ......I could buy you a cup of coffee one day this week to learn more about your field?
Option 2;......I could shadow you for a day and get a sense of what your day to day looks like?

Tom; Sure! I'd love to have coffee or you can even swing by the office this Friday and I'll show you around.

*Practical Application

Additionally, you can also request informational interviews with different hiring managers in the field you are researching. Again, just making connections with all these people and getting your name out there will assist you in learning more about the field/job you are researching. Secondly, the person you are interviewing may have a job or know someone else who has a position open. They would already be able to speak to your remarkable interview skills having done an informational interview with you already!

Finally, as you figure out what your dream job looks you need to ask yourself if you are an entrepreneur. This is sometimes the most overlooked area of the job search. I firmly believe that America was built for small businesses to succeed. If you have the financial stability, intestinal fortitude and basic business acumen needed to have a thriving business you could be the next Bill Gates!

We've talked a lot about "Why" you are looking for a dream job and now we have discussed what your dream may look like. Take your time in this section as it is very difficult to move forward to "The How" without being firmly rooted in the previous two sections.

Chapter Notes

What are your actions steps for this chapter?

_____

_____

_____

_____

_____

_____

_____

_____

_____

_____

_____

_____

_____

_____

_____

_____

_____

Chapter 4:
The HOW

Alright, this is what you've been waiting for!!!! Get excited, as we are about to find your DREAM JOB! I am passionate about what I do so I get a little excited sometimes. At this point in the process you should be coming to this section with an idea of what you have been called to do. There is a component of this dream job search that I don't take lightly and that is you passion. Passion can develop over time, but there should at least be a spark near a can of gasoline soaked wood. The thing we are about to find is the chance you have to change the world, the thing you are going to dedicate 1/3 of your non-sleeping hours towards, the thing that you should be excited to do when you have to do it late, do it early and do it day in and day out. If you don't have that thing, go back to Section 1&2 and find it, because past this point we only catch dreams!

We the information age upon us, social media is no passing fad. We need to embrace it, learn it, and utilize it for our advantage. Specifically, we need to have a basic understanding and knowledge of LinkedIn. No it is not too late to create a profile and jump on there. If you are on there we need to get you actually utilizing this wonderful tool. Think of LinkedIn as the 6 degrees of Kevin Bacon for any company or person you want to get connected too. If you are trying to meet a hiring manager in XYZ company, LinkedIn can help you see who you know that may already work there.

*Practical Application

Steps to getting your LinkedIn game on like Lebron!

1. Ensure you have a professional headshot in business attire suitable for your desired field.

2. Utilizing all of the people you know and email address book, request to connect with all your friends, family, former co-workers, church friends, chess club members, Toastmasters members, other clubs and organizations you are apart of.

3. Ensure all of your basic information is updated and accurate (schools, job history, etc.)

4. Develop a power statement as your intro line that speaks to what you are looking to transition into and highlight your skills.

5. Ensure you a well written Summary, Experience Skills section. The people you recently connected with will most likely start endorsing you for being amazing at whatever skills you list.

6. Follow the companies that you are interested in and see if already have connections (buy that connection a coffee and learn more about the organization).

7. Post articles that you find or create and get active on the site.

8. Join groups that professionals in your field are also members and be active in those groups to get more connections.

The above steps will get you started. Check out other peoples profiles and continue refining yours until you are really happy with the look and feel. I helped a person a few years ago get a job in a just under two weeks by doing steps 1-5 alone!

So we know our dream job, we need to decide if our current city supports this dream. Let's assume that it does and that you really like where you live your current school district. For the sake of this next piece we aren't moving. All this means is that our geography is fixed. With that in mind, you can probably find the 10 or 15 companies that fit your work criteria. Narrowed even further you may look at data that shows company size, specific location of offices in your neighborhood, etc. There are business journals and periodicals that can give you specific information regarding the top performing companies in your area.

*Practical Application

As adapted from 48 days to the Work You Love by Dan Miller. 6 job offers in 10 days

Step 1; Send and Introductory Letter on Day 1 to the hiring manager of dream companies 1-15 (snail mail)

- Clearly state your intentions and background on why they should give you the time of day
- Inform them that you will be sending your cover letter and resume in the next couple of days

Step 2; Send a cover letter and resume on Day 3 (snail mail)

- Make a resume specific to the duties and responsibilities for the role you are seeking or creating
- State that you will be calling in on X day at X time in your cover letter

Step 3; Make the call! on Day 5 (phone call not a text message or email)

- Thank them for taking the time to talk with you!
- Give your 30 second pitch
- Close the deal with a face to face meeting to discuss how you may be of value to their company

This process has led to me speaking to key decision makers having a conversation with me on getting hired for their company and secondary meetings to see if there was the possibility of a mutually beneficial situation. Managers are inundated with emails and meetings. I have found that regular mail still gets delivered and is perceived as

44

important since someone took the time to hand write their name and information on the envelope.

Last but not least, where are the brave ones? Where are the dreamers that want to start their own small business? This has been the scariest, most rewarding, most challenging, and did I say scariest thing I've ever done. This process is actually easier than you think and not as expensive as you think either. I've started businesses for less than $100 bucks and a box of business cards! Sometimes when people hear the word "business" they think of some big building on wall street. Well America has plenty of small businesses and the CEOs walk among you. They are the plumbers, the accountants, the pest control tech, the lawn care specialist, the financial advisor. Many of them don't advertise or sell, they build relationships and help people. We need to take away the fear factor of starting a business and the way I did this was three fold.

*Practical Application

- Create a good business plan
  - Research if your business idea is viable in your area
  - Speak with similar businesses in other cities about The Good, The Bad, and The Ugly of their industry
- Start small, start on the side

- This helps you maintain proper cash-flow during startup (Read the last bullet as; you won't starve and go broke during start-up)
- This also allows a little margin for error without having mortgaged your house to get your "life's dream" off the ground
  - No emotional blackmail allowed on your spouse for this dream to get going
- Start and stay Debt-Free
  - This is an entire book and theory all its own but still worth mentioning here. If you can't start your idea for less than $5,000 then you need to really evaluate the idea and see what piece you can start to get some money coming in the door
  - If you don't have $5K, just get it going with what you have and do what you can
  - Grow slowly and grow with CASH

Chapter Notes

What are your actions steps for this chapter?

_____

_____

_____

_____

_____

_____

_____

_____

_____

_____

_____

_____

_____

_____

_____

_____

_____

Conclusion

So you may have read this entire book and thought, where do we fill out 900 applications online or walk door to door to every business in our city. You can do that to find "A" job, but our goal was to find you your "Dream Job!" We need to be focused and intentional with our approach. This will help us save time and energy and heartache in the long run. Everything I have outlined is a tool in the tool box. I don't think there is one single tool that will lead you to the dream job. You have to use multiple tools to get this dream job built. We started this journey to give hope, empower people and give tools for finding their dream job. In all that we do we must have a WHY big enough to support the late nights, early mornings and adversity on the way to our dream. We must have a vision of WHAT we want. WHAT is your mission in life? WHAT is your passion? We must have a plan on HOW we will go about the business of achieving this dream.

I personally haven't achieved all my goals…YET. But I can proudly say that I am climbing the proverbial mountain and have reached the another summit. There are still higher heights but I can not discount the progress up the mountain that I have made thus far. I believe the same for you no matter what your situation. If you are at basecamp, then congratulations for gearing up and having a plan to start your climb. If you are on the climb, KEEP GOING! You have more cheerleaders than you know rooting for your success. If you have fallen, my advice is to learn from the past and improve your approach on your next attempt, and there had better be a next attempt! I'm rooting for you and I am on the journey with you!

Chapter Notes

What are you going to do with the tools you just received?   What is <u>your</u> plan for <u>your</u> career?

_____

_____

_____

_____

_____

_____

_____

_____

_____

_____

_____

_____

_____

_____

_____

_____

_____

NEXT STEPS

Resources

Friends, this is just the beginning! You need to stay plugged into a support system with accountability and encouragement. You are not alone in your journey. You can find other supporting resources at the following locations;

aaronlittles.com

- Here you will find books, downloadable content and my blog
- Additional if you need coaching you can get information there or email coaching@aaronlittles.com

Twitter

@aaronlittles

Speaking

If you lead a group that would find this material encouraging please contact:

booking@aaronlittles.com

Check out my speaking pages;

https://www.speakermatch.com/profile/aaronlittles/

http://mvpseminars.com/users/aaron_littles

www.ingramcontent.com/pod-product-compliance
Lightning Source LLC
Chambersburg PA
CBHW071644040426
42452CB00009B/1753